THE LITTLE BOOK OF

Aperitifs

50 CLASSIC COCKTAILS
AND DELIGHTFUL DRINKS

Kate Hawkings

Photography by Sarah Hogan

Hardie Grant

QUADRILLE

CONTENTS

INTRODUCTION

I was 12 when I first heard the word 'aperitif', at a chintzy country house hotel that reeked of uptight gentility and suppressed emotions. I was there to celebrate my great aunt Margaret's eightieth birthday. My parents, my older sister and I were ushered into the drawing room before dinner, Margaret gamely leading the way on her walking sticks, with her ill-fitting wig set at a jaunty angle. We perched on the over-stuffed sofas overloaded with cushions as leather-bound menus were flourished by the white-jacketed maitre d', sleek of hair and oleaginous of demeanour. Our host then uttered the immortal words, 'Would you care to commence with an aperitif?'

My sister issued a snort and my shoulders started shaking, but we managed to summon the good manners to wait until the poor man left the room before collapsing in hysterical giggles at this preposterous pomposity. When my father, who dined here occasionally with his clients, leaned towards us and whispered conspiratorially, 'His name is Mr Snodgrass,' we totally lost the plot, spluttering dry-roasted peanuts across the velvet pile carpet and crossing our legs tightly so we wouldn't wet our pants.

Our mother frowned and handed us the tissues she always carried in her handbag; we wiped the snot from our noses and regained a semblance of composure just as Mr Snodgrass returned with our drinks held aloft on a silver salver. Aunt Margaret said simply, 'Well, isn't this nice?'

It was bitter lemon for my sister and me – the go-to treat drink whenever it was on offer – while the ladies had Champagne and my father, a Campari Soda. The drinks arrived in immaculate crystal glassware, a ramrod-stiff linen coaster deftly placed beneath each one by the fawning Mr S. He produced his pen and notebook with a flourish. 'And may I take your order for dinner?' At that moment a passion in my heart was born for the aperitif – the very word, the sense of occasion, and my-oh-my, the drinks.

Campari Soda is my absolute favourite aperitif; from time to time I replace the soda with bitter lemon and drink in homage to dear Mr Snodgrass.

The word 'aperitif' comes from the Latin *aperire*, meaning 'to open'. It is something to open the appetite, to stimulate the taste buds, to mark the start of a meal that's to come. It could be a perfect gin and tonic before a long and louche lunch that ends the wrong side of midnight, a Martini to flex the digestive muscles at the start of a dinner out with friends, or perhaps a glass of something lovely at a bar on your way home for supper.

More usually for most of us, an aperitif is what properly announces the opening of the evening at home at the end of a long day when we turn our attention to the important things in life – perhaps cooking, eating, drinking and talking with the one or ones we love, or just slugging something into a glass, making cheese on toast and snuggling up solo with friends on social media. Some cocktails can be considered aperitifs, and Champagne certainly counts; a glass of wine can't put a foot wrong if it has a crispy pizazz to get your juices flowing and a snifter of sherry will always suit, but *apéros*, as the French fondly call them, can be so much more.

Many of the classic aperitifs date back centuries and have their roots in medicinal compounds that all manner of chemists, alchemists, quacks and clergy concocted using whatever nearby nature offered. Such drinks were usually devised to aid digestion; water was often contaminated and food hygiene standards were slack, so the digestive health of populations needed

all the help it could get. Where there's medicine, there's money, particularly if the tincture tasted good, so making snifters to be taken before eating became big business.

The histories of many of these drinks are lost in the mists and alcoholic daze of yore; others are newer to the aperitif party, the result of the vogue in the drinking business to resurrect and revive forgotten recipes as well as to use them as inspiration for new drinks for the modern age.

Aperitifs occupy a particular niche in drinking land. Cocktails are all well and good in the drinker's repertoire, but the aperitif suggests something rather lighter, something to tickle one's fancy without wrestling one's taste buds and sobriety into submission. There is a trend towards drinking lighter alcohol and less of it, and the aperitif vibe fits this bill perfectly. Also, they don't need the hand of a skilled bartender so are easy to knock up at home.

Sharpeners, snifters, aperitivos or noggins (my granny's word, and perhaps my favourite): we all know what we mean. Let us raise a glass to the aperitif, that most civilised and cheering of drinking habits.

GIN

GIN & TONIC

||||||||||||||||||||||||||||||||||||||||||||||||||||||||||||

50ml/2fl oz gin
150ml/6fl oz tonic
slice of lemon, wedge of lime or perhaps a fine strip of cucumber

The very making of a G&T is an act to make the spirit soar. The clink-clink-clink of ice cubes tumbling into a spotless glass, the satisfying twist of opening the bottle, then the glug-glug as the gin goes in. 'Psst' goes the tonic in an inviting manner when you open it, then the joyous bubbles cascade, tickling our noses when we get up close. Add an invigorating spritz of citrus and it's like liquid music in transparent form.

There is good reason that the gin and tonic could be said to be the apogee of aperitifs: not only is it a thing of great aesthetic beauty, it ticks all the physiological aperitif boxes as well. The alcohol in the gin cleans the tongue of lunch's debris while the underlying bitterness of its botanicals sets off alarm bells in our brains to get digestive juices flowing sharpish, and along with that comes the frisson of subconscious danger and its accompanying endorphin high. Tonic's quinine bitterness only intensifies the hit. Then come the bubbles – their tickling sensation on the tongue also encourages salivation – while the acidity of citrus makes it a hat trick.

There is a fashion, coming from the gin-loving Spaniards, to serve G&Ts in big, goldfish bowl-shaped glasses. They certainly can look impressive, but I have my reservations. Firstly, they're quite hard to hold. You end up clutching them with all your fingers and possibly some palm, which transfers heat and thus warms the drink. Plenty of ice is essential to mitigate such damage and you want it to last until you've reached the bottom of the glass, so we're talking serious volumes of ice here compared to that of liquid. In addition, the wide mouth of these goblets makes the bubbles of the tonic dissipate more quickly, and the fizz is most definitely part of the fun. Also, the Spanish are far more generous when it comes to their measures – not for them the use of a jigger; they free-pour gin with gusto, unlike the uptight and law-abiding Brits whose G&Ts made in this fashion will almost certainly mean their miserly measures of gin will be beaten into submission by the quantities of ice and tonic used to make the drink look right.

In a bar I want the drink made in front of me, with the glass filled with ice first and the gin poured on top. I like to be asked what garnish I prefer – usually lemon, though lime is more modish, occasionally a twirl of cucumber skin. If the flesh of the citrus is rubbed around the rim before being dropped in the glass, so much the better.

My tonic should always be served in a small bottle or, even better, a can – never, ever those hateful guns – and I don't mind the bartender adding a little tonic to the glass then leaving the rest of the bottle alongside, but WOE BETIDE anybody who has the audacity to pour in the tonic up to the top of the glass. How very dare they assume they know how I like my dilution? It's very easy for the gin to be overpowered by the tonic; I like to taste it first as a one-to-one mixture then add extra tonic as I see fit.

And yes, I might (or might not) like a straw, perhaps two, instead of an irritating plastic stirrer that just gets in the way after it's done its job. (Having said that, I was once served a superlative G&T in George Clooney's suite in a smart hotel in the Italian alps. Tragically, George was not there at the time but the drink came with an exquisite stirrer, a long droplet of clear Murano glass that was an utter joy to use, first to stir the drink and then to lick before laying it down gently on the linen napkin. Reader, I stole it.)

The straw allows for gentle stirring and subsequent sipping, but a word of warning here: over-stirring will make the bubbles disperse quickly and flatten the tonic so use your straw and/or stirrer with caution.

At home I favour small cans of tonic (and yes, for me, it has to be Schweppes), over the larger individual bottles. These cans contain 150ml, which is just about right with a 50ml shot of gin. Large bottles of tonic just lose their fizz too quickly, and anyway seem flatter to start with than tonic from a can or small bottle. They may seem a cheaper option but unless you're serving six G&Ts at a time, they're generally a false economy.

MARTINI

10 parts gin
1 part vermouth
twist of lemon or a green olive, to garnish

Professional boozehounds agree to differ when it comes to their favoured proportions of gin to vermouth, and when it comes to which brands they use. This is my preferred recipe for a dry Martini, using 50ml No3 London Dry gin and a teaspoon (5ml) of Noilly Prat vermouth. Fill a cocktail shaker or a jug with ice, then pour in the gin and the vermouth. Stir with a cocktail spoon for no longer than ten seconds then strain into a chilled (very important) cocktail glass. Garnish with a twist of lemon or a green olive. It should, as one anonymous writer noted, resemble Fred Astaire in a glass.

VARIATIONS

Dirty Martini	Add a splash of olive brine, garnish with an olive
Gibson	Garnish with a cocktail onion
Pink Martini	Add a splash of Angostura bitters
Churchill Martini	No vermouth; simply stir the gin over the ice to chill and slightly dilute it and serve with an olive marinated in dry vermouth
Dripping (or wet) Martini	Half-and-half gin and vermouth
Burnt Martini	Add a splash of a peaty whisky
Bradford	A shaken Martini (so called, rather unfairly to Bradford, that bluff town in Yorkshire, because it's always cloudy)
Parisienne	Add half a teaspoon of crème de cassis

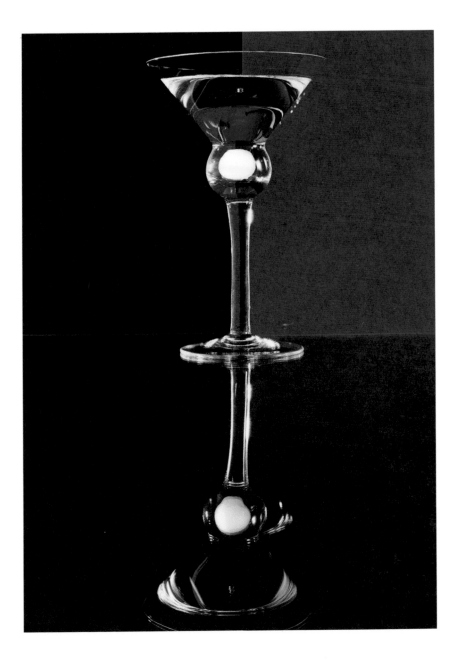

The American writer H.L. Mencken claimed the Martini is 'the only American invention as perfect as the sonnet'. Quite a claim, but one that quite possibly stands up for the seasoned drinker, for a good Martini is an aperitif of great, if potentially dangerous, joy.

It's impossible to verify who invented the Martini – some claim it was Jerry Thomas, author of the seminal *Bar-Tender's Guide* of 1862, in San Francisco's Occidental Hotel for a miner from the town of Martinez in California who had struck gold and was in the mood to celebrate. Others say that it was a bartender named Martini di Arma di Taggia at New York's Knickerbocker Hotel in the early 20th century. Or was it just a shortening of a 'Martini and gin' – Martini & Rossi being a brand of Italian vermouth first produced in 1863? Whatever.

What we do know is that by the 1920s, the Martini had become the cocktail *du jour*, and its further associations with glamorous and celebrated drinkers – Dorothy Parker, Ernest Hemingway, F. Scott Fitzgerald, Marlene Dietrich, and Humphrey Bogart – ensured its popularity continued to grow.

In the days of prohibition in America, gin was distilled illegally and was notoriously foul of flavour. The addition of vermouth made it more palatable and the drink added up to something much more than the sum of its parts. The original recipe was likely to be something close to half and half (known as a wet Martini; the more vermouth you use, the 'wetter' it becomes), but as the quality of gin improved in the following decades, the fashion became for the drinks to become drier by holding back on the vermouth and upping the gin. This does, it should be noted, also make the drink more alcoholic. Martinis became even drier in the UK and America during WWII as exports of Italian and French vermouths dried up during Nazi occupation.

Noël Coward was another Martini lover, and he liked them very, very dry. His recipe was to 'fill a glass with gin and wave it in the general direction of Italy', while Winston Churchill's advice was to merely whisper the word 'vermouth' as you drank the gin. I'm also rather partial to Julia Child's 'reverse Martini' – a glass of Noilly Prat vermouth over ice with a splash of gin on top. Recommended for daytime drinking or when there's a need to err on the side of caution.

Most bartenders would agree that James Bond, another famous imbiber, was mistaken in his request for his Martini to be 'shaken not stirred' – shaking the ingredients makes the drink cloudy.

However you take your Martinis, I urge you to heed Dorothy Parker's dictum: I have put it to the test on more than one ill-judged occasion and can vouch for its good sense.'I love to drink Martinis, but two at the very most. After three I'm under the table, after four I'm under the host.'

CHARLIE CHAPLIN

◇◇◇◇◇◇◇◇◇◇◇◇◇◇◇◇◇◇◇◇◇◇◇◇◇◇◇◇◇◇◇◇

juice of half a lime
25ml/1fl oz sloe gin
25ml/1fl oz apricot brandy

Mix the ingredients over ice in a tumbler.

Sloe gin is such a lovely thing to have
in your possession. A bag of berries
from hawthorn bushes foraged on an
autumn walk are mixed with sugar and
gin, then left to work their magic just
in time for Christmas. The result is a
sweet-but-sharp tincture that can be
sipped at pretty much any time of day
and lasts for months once it's bottled.
If you don't have the time or inclination
to make your own, there are plenty of
good sloe gins to buy in the shops.

You can mix it with tonic or ginger beer
to make a long drink, or use it in this
classic recipe, named for the famous
silent film actor and director. The
correct way is to strain it and serve in a
chilled cocktail glass, but I like it just as
much made in this more slapdash way.

BAR TERMINI'S
MARSALA MARTINI

IIIIIIIIIIIIIIIIIIIIIIIIIIIIIIIIIIIIIIIIIIIIIIIIIIIIIIIIIIIIIIIIIII

50ml/2fl oz gin (Bar Termini uses Beefeater)
12.5ml/½fl oz dry marsala
½ tsp dry vermouth (Martini Extra Dry is my preference)
1 dash orange bitters (Bar Termini makes its own almond bitters)

To make the pickled almonds:
12 skinned, blanched almonds
about 150ml/5fl oz Champagne or cider vinegar
1 tsp salt

For the pickled almonds, put the almonds in a small jar or bowl.
Cover with Champagne or cider vinegar, stir in the salt gently until it
has dissolved, then leave covered for 24 hours. Drain off the liquid and
set the almonds aside (they will keep for 2 weeks in an airtight tin).

Stir the ingredients over plenty of ice just enough to chill them – ten stirs
should do it. Strain into a beautiful glass, drop in a pickled almond, stand
back and watch your guests swoon. Mamma mia.

Tony Conigliaro is a shining star in
the London cocktail firmament whose
killer drinks have been making serious
drinkers go weak at the knees for years.
He is the brains behind Bar Termini,
a tiny bar on Old Compton Street in
Soho modelled on the bar at the train
station in Rome. This is my favourite of
his many splendid drinks. The pickled
almond is essential to the drink: a jewel
to be scraped out of the bottom of the
glass with your finger and eaten with
the final swig of this very clever aperitif,
so you do need to plan ahead, but only
by 24 hours or thereabouts.

GIN AND IT

◇◇◇◇◇◇◇◇◇◇◇◇◇◇◇◇◇◇◇◇◇◇◇◇◇◇◇◇◇

50ml/2fl oz gin
50ml/2fl oz Martini Rosso
griotte cherries, to garnish

**Stir the gin and Martini over ice and strain into a chilled coupe.
Garnish with griotte cherries.**

The Gin and It – gin and Italian vermouth – is one of my favourite cocktails of all. It appears in many old movies and novels, but inexplicably seems to have fallen out of favour.

They were a favourite of the late and very great Dick Bradsell, the man credited with singlehandedly reviving the British cocktail scene in the 1980s and beyond, bringing to the bar proper, grown-up tinctures that continue to make our hearts beat that little bit faster. This is the man who gave the world the Bramble, the Treacle, the Pink Chihuahua and, perhaps most famously of all, the Espresso Martini. The latter was invented for a certain young supermodel who asked him to make her 'something that will wake me up, then fuck me up'. Dick, the consummate pro, gave his customer just what she wanted.

In the 1950s, the Gin and It was probably two measures of gin to one of vermouth, served with ice in a tumbler, but this is Dick's version. It's a very versatile drink – try experimenting with different gins and vermouths in different proportions.

A Gin and It is essentially a Martini (though probably pre-dates it), but made with sweet (red) vermouth rather than the usual dry (white). I've dabbled with vermouth styles in between and can happily report that gin mixed with some of the richer white vermouths can make a very happy marriage, especially when garnished with a sprig of mint or perhaps some thyme. Stir over ice and strain if you wish, but this kind of drink also takes kindly to being knocked up in a tumbler on the rocks in a domestic setting.

PINK GIN

//

6 drops of Angostura bitters
50ml/2fl oz gin

Slosh the Angostura bitters into a tumbler and swirl it around so that it coats the sides. Add as much gin as you fancy. Chuck in a couple of ice cubes and there you have it.

Whoever drinks Pink Gin these days? Who even knows what it is? Well, I do. It can lay claim to be one of the world's earliest cocktails, though 'cocktail' seems rather too fancy a word for a drink that is so simple.

Dating from around 1826 when HMS Hercules was patrolling the waters of the Caribbean, the Pink Gin came about when the ship's surgeon Henry Workshop came across Angostura bitters on one of his forays ashore.

Angostura contains antimalarial quinine but is far too bitter to be taken alone. Captain Jack Bristol added it to his evening gin and discovered it was rare good. He would probably have had no ice, but that doesn't mean you need to go without.

GIMLET

||||||||||||||||||||||||||||||||||||||||||||||||||||||||||||||

50ml/2fl oz gin
35ml/1½fl oz Rose's Lime juice Cordial

Serve in a tumbler over plenty of ice; no garnish required.

Scurvy was the scourge of sailors when European explorers sailed the seas in centuries past. A disease caused by lack of vitamin C, scurvy results in a slow and unpleasant death and it devastated crews on long voyages until, in the mid-18th century, it was discovered that citrus fruits helped keep scurvy at bay. Lemons and limes were carried on board, hence 'limey', the slang word for British seamen. In 1867, Lauchlin Rose, owner of a shipyard in Scotland, developed a recipe for lime juice preserved with sugar: Rose's Lime Juice Cordial was born and consequently saved the lives of countless seamen. Sailors mixed it with their daily rations of rum and water to make grog, while the officers preferred to mix it with neat gin.

In Raymond Chandler's 1954 novel *The Long Goodbye*, his hard-drinking private eye hero Philip Marlowe was a keen drinker of Gimlets, which were also Chandler's tipple of choice. 'Half gin and half Rose's Lime Cordial and nothing else,' is the recipe given in the book; he is quite specific that it should not contain fresh lime juice, as is now modish, though made in his way the drink is quite sweet for modern tastes, so I hold back on the cordial and up the gin. I think the fashion to use fresh lime juice in place of Rose's, somehow implying that it is morally superior, takes it into the realms of becoming a daiquiri and so rather defeats the point – a Gimlet is one of my store-cupboard cocktails, one that can be knocked up easily from ingredients I always have to hand. 'It beats Martinis hollow,' as the great detective said.

WINE &
FORTIFIED WINE

KÜMMEL SPRITZ

◇◇◇◇◇◇◇◇◇◇◇◇◇◇◇◇◇◇◇◇◇◇◇◇◇◇◇◇◇

25ml/1fl oz kümmel liqueur
125ml/4½fl oz robust white wine, chilled
soda water
orange slice

**Mix the kümmel and the wine together in a wine glass,
add a few cubes of ice, top with soda water, then
squeeze the orange slice as you drop it into the glass.**

Kümmel is a curious liqueur. Flavoured with caraway, cumin and fennel, it's sweet and syrupy yet herbaceously astringent, floral but with an earthy, spicy underbelly, and pretty strong at 38% abv. Thought to have been first made by the Dutch in 1575, kümmel caught the eye of the Peter the Great in 1696 when he was living incognito in the Netherlands learning shipbuilding skills. He took the liqueur back to Russia where he introduced it to the imperial court, and it became a firm favourite of that country as a digestif and general pick-me-up.

The most famous (and my favourite) brand is Mentzendorff, originally made in Riga on the Baltic coast and brought to Britain in 1851 by Ludwig Mentzendorff, whose wine-importing business is still going strong. Today it is made to the original recipe at the Combier Distillery in France in stills designed by Gustave Eiffel (of Tower fame).

I drink kümmel rarely, but when I do, I really love it. It stands well in cocktails with bracing backbones of strong, dry liquor; a Silver Bullet is good (twice as much dry gin to kümmel with a little lemon juice, either shaken with ice and strained into a cocktail glass, or just mixed in a tumbler on the rocks), but I prefer a Bearskin Martini (75ml vodka, 10ml kümmel, 10ml dry vermouth, treated as above), not least because it has a better name.

But this drink is something else, the result of a happy, slightly squiffy accident. I'd been tasting kümmel from a wine glass (in a professional capacity, I should add) and absentmindedly left the glass on my kitchen worktop at the end of the day. I was chatting with a friend as we cooked dinner together later, drinking a very nice chardonnay from the Jura region. As the night wore on my friend gallantly topped up our glasses, accidentally pouring the wine into the kümmel. We tasted it in trepidation and with morbid fascination – in theory, this should be a catastrophe in a glass – but were astonished to discover it actually works very well, although it definitely needs the orange and the soda to lift it. Expensive wine from Jura is frankly wasteful, but do use something with a bit of body to carry the weight of the kümmel – an inexpensive lightly oaked chardonnay would be perfect.

TINTO DE VERANO

||||||||||||||||||||||||||||||||||||||||||||||||||||||||||||||

1 part red wine
2 parts lemonade, soda and/or tonic water
1 lemon slice

Pour the wine into a tumbler or tall glass, add a few cubes of ice, then top up with either a mixture of lemonade and soda, or tonic water. Squeeze the lemon slice as you drop it into the glass.

Meaning 'summer red wine', this Spanish favourite is great way to use up red wine that's past its prime. It's a humble drink that's fitting for a sunny day, and one that's relatively low in alcohol (something to bear in mind when boozing under a blazing sun). Soda water cuts the sweetness of lemonade, while tonic makes an agreeably bitter alternative. The lemon slice adds a lifting zestiness.

WINE & FORTIFIED WINE

BICICLETTA

◇◇◇◇◇◇◇◇◇◇◇◇◇◇◇◇◇◇◇◇◇◇◇◇◇◇◇◇◇

splash of Campari
dry white wine
soda water (optional)
lemon slice, to garnish

Slosh the Campari into a wine glass and top up with chilled white wine.
Add a splash of soda water if liked. Garnish with a slice of lemon.

A generous slug of Campari with
white wine in a wine glass and perhaps
a splash of soda water: the Bicicletta is
a classic and very easy Italian aperitif
with very good reason. Supposedly
named in acknowledgement of the
gentlemen who'd weave home on their
bicycles after one too many at their
local bar, it's a nifty way of covering the
shame of a dreary pinot grigio or other
cheap white wine. Don't drown it out
with too much soda; just make sure the
Campari and wine come straight from
the fridge. Another store-cupboard
aperitif for which it's easy to develop
a taste.

FINO AND FIZZ

IIIIIIIIIIIIIIIIIIIIIIIIIIIIIIIIIIIIIIIIIIIIIIIIIIIIIIIIIIII

50ml/2fl oz fino sherry
15ml/¹/₃fl oz apricot liqueur
soda water
1 sprig basil and 1 green olive, to garnish

Mix the sherry and liqueur in a large wine glass, add plenty
of ice and top with soda water. Give it a stir then garnish
with a sprig of basil and a green olive.

Shamelessly lifted from Ryan
Chetiyawardana's book *Good Things to
Drink* (he calls his drink Bubbles and
Byass), this shows how brilliantly dry
sherry can work in a long drink. Any
cheap and cheerful fino will do, or try it
with amontillado for more nutty depth.

REBUJITO

///

75ml/3fl oz manzanilla or fino sherry
about 150ml/6fl oz lemonade
1 sprig fresh mint and/or 1 green olive, to garnish

Serve in a tall glass over plenty of ice.

This classic Andalusian aperitif uses
manzanilla or fino sherry and is fantastic
in the summer; use an amontillado or
an oloroso instead for something a bit
more profound but equally delicious
and more fitting for winter. Spanish
lemonade is somewhat less sweet than
those the Brits and Americans are used
to, so I'd top it with a splash of soda to
cut the sweetness. I sometimes throw
caution to the wind and use tonic water
instead of lemonade.

PORT AND GINGER

||||||||||||||||||||||||||||||||||||||||||||||||||||||||

50ml/2fl oz red port
150ml/6fl oz ginger ale
a fat lemon slice

**Pour the port into a tall glass with some ice. Top up
with ginger ale and squeeze the lemon slice over the top.**

Port is one of those things that
tends to lurk around for weeks after
Christmas, its starring role with the
festive cheeseboard long forgotten.
Red ports – ruby, vintage and LBV
– oxidise and spoil quite quickly after
opening and this is a good way to
extend their life a little.

Inspired by the Port and Lemon (ruby
port mixed with lemonade), a staple
'ladies' drink' in beery pubs half a
century ago, it replaces the lemonade
with ginger ale to add a little spicy
kick; the lemon is essential to cut the
sweetness of the drink.

WHITE WINE SANGRIA

◇◇◇◇◇◇◇◇◇◇◇◇◇◇◇◇◇◇◇◇◇◇◇◇◇◇◇◇

Makes enough for six thirsty people on a sunny day
1 bottle (70cl/25fl oz) cheap white wine
125ml/4½fl oz triple sec or marmalade vodka (see page 75)
600ml/21fl oz ginger beer
300ml/10½fl oz soda
peach slices, raspberries and mint sprigs, to garnish

**In a large jug (or two smaller ones), mix the wine and triple sec.
Add ice, top up with the ginger beer and soda, garnish with the
peach slices and mint sprigs and serve in tall glasses.**

I use the term 'sangria' loosely here.
Usually made with red wine, lemonade,
orange juice and brandy, and served
with no-holds-barred quantities of
chopped fruit, sangria first took off as
a by-the-jug sundowner with tourists
in Spain decades ago and is still a
popular drink to serve at summer
parties. Without wishing to be rude,
it generally makes my heart sink – the
tannins in the wine loudly clashing with
the orange juice, the lemonade making
it sickly sweet rather than refreshing,
and the brandy ensuring a thumping
headache by the time you get to bed.

This is more restrained – but still packs
a get-the-party-started punch.

WHITE PORT & TONIC

◇◇◇◇◇◇◇◇◇◇◇◇◇◇◇◇◇◇◇◇◇◇◇◇◇◇◇◇◇◇

75ml/3fl oz white port
tonic water
a slice or wedge of lemon, to garnish
a sprig of rosemary, to garnish

Pour the white port into a tall glass over ice. Top up with tonic water to taste, and garnish with the lemon and rosemary.

I tip my hat to a band called the Four Deuces who recorded a song in 1956 called 'WPLJ' – white port and lemon juice – which was later covered by Frank Zappa. No recipe is given in the lyrics but I read it as a comfortable sufficiency of white port slugged over ice with a generous wedge of lemon to squeeze over it. As the chorus to the song so aptly puts it:

I feel so good
I feel so fine
I got plenty lovin'
And I got plenty wine.

Having said that, I treat white port in the same way as I do with most pale fortified wines: lovely chilled alone or over some ice, or sensationally delicious when mixed with tonic in this way.

White port and tonic can handle all sorts of garnishes – I tinker happily with thyme, basil, mint or even cinnamon; but I love the rasping austerity of rosemary. Lemon is always my citrus of choice.

FIRST OF THE SUMMER WINE

||||||||||||||||||||||||||||||||||||||||||||||||||||||||||||||

50ml/2fl oz gin
20ml/³/₄fl oz tawny port
2 tsp lemon juice
tonic water
mint leaves, thyme and orange slices, to garnish

Take a high-ball glass, or something similar, load it with ice and sling in the gin. Pour over the port and the lemon juice, give it a stir, then top up with tonic. Go large on the garnish – some mint leaves, a sprig of thyme and a generous slice of orange.

This is from one of my favourite bars in the world, Hausbar in Bristol, where German-born Aurelius Braunbarth brought Berlin basement bar chic to the fortunate few and has never been bettered, in Bristol at least. Gone but very much not forgotten, in 12 years of glorious rule Auri and his much-feted protégées at Hausbar made me so many perfect drinks I'd never attempt to recreate at home, such is the skill and attention to critical detail with which they were made. This one is easy to knock up at home; 'It's just a posh G&T,' says Auri, with characteristic cool. Choose whatever gin you like, bearing in mind you don't want to overpower the gorgeous, delicate fruitiness of the port.

SPARKLING WINE

BLACK VELVET

◇◇◇◇◇◇◇◇◇◇◇◇◇◇◇◇◇◇◇◇◇◇◇◇◇◇◇◇◇◇◇◇

2 x 440ml/15½fl oz cans Guinness or stout
1 bottle (70cl/25fl oz) Champagne or sparkling wine

Mix equal quantities of well-chilled Guinness (or stout of your choice) and Champagne (or other sparkling wine) together in a jug. Pour into 12 Champagne flutes, tilting the glasses as you go to prevent it frothing over.

Is it an aperitif? Or is it a first course in itself? A Black Velvet is cold and refreshing – as an aperitif should be – yet it also feels nourishing to both body and soul (it must be all that health-giving iron in the Guinness).

Said to have been invented to mark the death of Queen Victoria's husband, Prince Albert, in 1861, the Black Velvet is as luxurious and rich and smooth as its namesake and oozes a kind of gothic glamour. It's also incredibly simple to make.

It suits to kick off one of those late Sunday lunches with friends in the winter that you just know will go on a little too late. Champagne is used in the classic recipe, but it wouldn't suffer much if made with cheap fizz.

BELLINI
AND VARIOUS FIZZY COUSINS

||||||||||||||||||||||||||||||||||||||||||||||||||||||||||

100ml/4fl oz white peach purée
1 bottle (70cl/25fl oz) sparkling wine

Stir the purée and wine together in a jug.
Pour slowly into chilled flutes, stirring gently as you go.

The classic Bellini, invented by Giuseppe Cipriani in 1948 at Venice's famous Harry's Bar and named after the 15th-century painter Giovanni Bellini, takes white peach purée and tops it up with prosecco.

Make your own purée by poaching very ripe peaches in a little water then straining through a fine sieve (sweeten it a little, if you like). Other summer fruits work well treated the same way – try raspberries, strawberries, blackcurrants or (my favourite) redcurrants. When autumn hits try blackberries, and in the depths of winter use rhubarb. Fruit liqueurs such as crème de cassis (blackcurrant), crème de mûre (blackberry) or even apricot brandy are a handy standby, and damson and sloe gin also work well.

Red vermouths rub along nicely with sparkling wine, and to my mind make brilliant aperitifs as their appetising bitterness broods in the background of the fruity bubbles. About 20ml/¾fl oz of vermouth in the bottom of a flute should do it, although the weight and intensity of your vermouth may mean you want to go lower or higher.

If I'm drinking decent fizz, it seems rather like gilding the lily to add anything else to its classy finesse. Sparkling wines of a more lowly pedigree, however, often respond well to a little gilding. Cheap fizz can be punishingly acidic after a glass or two, yet its edges can be so easily softened to give drinks real pizazz. Be aware that prosecco tends to have an underlying sweetness to it while cava is usually drier, so you may want to adjust things accordingly.

CAMPARI CORRETTO

25ml/1fl oz Campari
125ml/4¼fl oz sparkling wine
a few drops of orange bitters (optional)

Pour the Campari into a flute and top up with sparkling wine.
The orange bitters are entirely optional but they do transform this
drink into something rather sublime.

Campari Corretto (meaning 'corrected')
is a riff on the Bellini that uses Campari
in place of the peach purée. I've
selflessly tested this at some length
and can report that it's best with a
heavy hand on the Campari so that its
personality stands out amid all
the sparkles.

FRENCH 75

◇◇◇◇◇◇◇◇◇◇◇◇◇◇◇◇◇◇◇◇◇◇◇◇◇◇◇◇

35–50ml/1½–2fl oz London dry gin
  (depending on how strong you're feeling)
1 tbsp lemon juice
1 tsp caster (superfine) sugar
  (or 1 tsp sugar syrup, should you have some to hand)
125ml/4¼fl oz sparkling wine
a twist of lemon

To make the drink properly, mix 'enough' dry gin with the lemon juice and sugar (or sugar syrup) in a cocktail shaker until the sugar has dissolved. Add a few cubes of ice and stir for 10 seconds, then strain into a flute. Alternatively, just sling the gin, lemon juice and sugar into whatever glass you have to hand and give it a stir. Top up with sparkling wine and add a twist of lemon.

This drink has evolved from the Soixante-Quinze, created in 1915 and named because it was so strong it feels like being shot with a French 75mm field gun, capable of firing 15 rounds per minute. Originally made with gin, apple brandy, grenadine and lemon juice, in 1926 Harry MacElhone, an American bartender in Paris, took a riff on it with gin, Calvados, grenadine and absinthe, and dubbed it the '75'.

Harry Craddock, in his 1930 *The Savoy Cocktail Book*, gives the recipe above (but serves it on the rocks) and calls it the 'French 75'. His one comment is: 'Hits with remarkable precision'. You have been warned.

'CHAMPAGNE' COCKTAIL

|||||||||||||||||||||||||||||||||||||||||||||||||||||||||

1 white sugar cube
3–4 drops of Angostura bitters
25ml/1fl oz brandy
125ml/4¼fl oz Champagne or sparkling wine

Place the sugar cube in the base of a flute and add the Angostura bitters and brandy. Top with well-chilled fizz and away you go.

In a similar vein to the French 75, but with brandy in place of the gin, this drink is simpler and marginally less dangerous. I've no idea what Diana Dors drank, but for some reason this reminds me of her – a bit over the top and rather blousy, but jolly good fun at a party.

SPRITZ

◇◇◇◇◇◇◇◇◇◇◇◇◇◇◇◇◇◇◇◇◇◇◇◇◇◇◇◇◇◇◇

75ml/3fl oz prosecco or sparkling wine
50ml/2fl oz Aperol or other amaro
25ml/1fl oz (just a splash) soda
slice of orange or lemon, to garnish

**Combine the prosecco, Aperol and soda over ice in a large wine glass
or chunky tumbler. Garnish with a slice of lemon or orange.**

The Venetians can arguably lay claim to have invented the spritz – originally made with local amaro and white wine and lengthened with soda, ideal to take the edge off the thirst at the end of a hot summer's day.

Aperol's masterful marketing brought the drink to the grateful masses in the early 2000s and Aperol Spritz is now Venice's favourite aperitif. Their easy-to-remember 3:2:1 prosecco:Aperol:soda recipe is a pretty good benchmark, although I encourage you to experiment with things other than Aperol: Campari, of course, as well as Cynar, but red vermouths with a bit of oomph can work really well too – try Antica Formula or Punt e Mes.

The important thing is to retain the integrity of the base drink – too much prosecco and/or soda will render your spritz weak and dreary. And the wine needn't necessarily be prosecco – cava works just as well and is less sweet, or use an un-fizzy, workaday white wine for something somewhat less spritzy but still charming.

VERMOUTH

VERMOUTHS ALONE IN
ALL THEIR GLORY

Much as I love a Negroni or a good Martini, a Gin and It or a Cardinale, I really enjoy drinking vermouths alone, chilled from the fridge with maybe some ice and a slice of lemon, lime or orange. I learnt to drink vermouth this way in Barcelona almost a decade ago when an art historian I'd met in Gaudí's astonishingly bonkers Sagrada Família cathedral took me down an alley and introduced me to the Spanish way of drinking what they call vermuts. I was totally hooked and remain so to this day.

White or red, they charm me both, though the Spanish tend to favour the red. It's a drink to sip and enjoy at leisure: its bitterness really wakes up the taste buds and its intense botanicals always intrigue. Orange is the most usual garnish in Spain, along with a fat green olive on a stick whose salty notes give a dashing finish to the drink. Lemon or lime often suit dry vermouths better but there are really no rules to follow. Consider the characteristics of your chosen vermouth/vermut and pick something you think might suit.

MANHATTAN

||||||||||||||||||||||||||||||||||||||||||||||||||||||

2 parts rye whiskey
1 part red vermouth
a few dashes of Angostura bitters
maraschino cherry, to garnish

Stir together the whiskey and vermouth in a tumbler or cocktail shaker over ice, and add a few dashes of Angostura bitters. Strain into a chilled cocktail glass, garnished with a maraschino cherry.

A Manhattan appears here because it is one of the classic vermouth cocktails, though it's one I rarely make at home; I prefer to drink it in a darkened bar with the promise of a debauched night ahead. Very *Mad Men*.

NEGRONI SBAGLIATO

◇◇◇◇◇◇◇◇◇◇◇◇◇◇◇◇◇◇◇◇◇◇◇◇◇◇◇

25ml/1fl oz Campari
25ml/1fl oz red vermouth
125ml/4¼fl oz sparkling wine
orange slice, to garnish (optional)

Pour the Campari and vermouth into a tumbler or flute and top up with fizz.

This is a riff on a Negroni, 'sbagliato' meaning 'incorrect'. It was supposedly invented by a barman in Bar Basso in Milan when he inadvertently reached for the prosecco and not the gin.

As with so many of these drinks, the vermouth you choose is up to you. Martini Rosso is the standard here but I rather like it with something a bit lighter – Regal Rogue's Bold Red vermouth really rocks my boat.

Some people serve Sbagliati in flutes but I prefer a tumbler with ice and a slice of orange, just as in a classic Negroni.

While we're on the subject of substitutions in classic Negronis, if you replace the gin with tequila you have a Jalisco Negroni; swap the gin for rum and it becomes a Kingston Negroni. And if you're feeling very brave, simply replace the Campari with a teaspoon (no more) of Fernet Branca and you have an approximation of a Hanky Panky, mentioned here as a nod to Ada Coleman, who invented it in around 1920 when she was head bartender at London's Savoy Hotel. Attagirl, Ada.

SUZE NEGRONI

///

25ml/1fl oz gin
25ml/1fl oz white vermouth or something a bit fruity
*   such as Lillet Blanc or Cocchi Americano Bianco*
25ml/1fl oz Suze
wedge of lime or bergamot, to serve

Build as per a normal Negroni, over ice in chunky tumbler. If you happen
to have a bergamot to hand, a twist of its knobbly peel would only add to
the drink's exotic appeal. Lime would work fine if you don't.

Suze has a wonderful fragrant, floral
bitterness and here takes the place
of Campari, while white vermouth
is there instead of the red. Like all
Negronis, this is pretty pokey if made to
standard strength as above; if I'm feeling
abstemious, I might make a smaller
quantity, perhaps using the cap of a
bottle as a measure (which holds about
10ml) mixed in a little glass, and that
generally hits the spot. I might have
another if it doesn't.

CARDINALE

|||||||||||||||||||||||||||||||||||||||||||||||||||||||||||

1 part Campari
1 part gin
1 part dry white vermouth
lemon peel, to garnish

**Pour the Campari, gin and vermouth over ice in a tumbler
and garnish with lemon peel.**

Put simply, this is a Negroni that
substitutes the red vermouth with
white. Recipes vary as to proportions;
the classic 1:1:1 generally works for
me, though it's worth experimenting
depending on what gin and vermouth
you're using.

I'd stick to a London dry gin, probably
Beefeater, but my choice of vermouth
would depend on how I'm feeling and
what I've got in my cocktail cupboard.
Noilly Prat or Martini Extra Dry
will lend the classic Cardinale vibe;
something a bit richer such as Cocchi
Americano bianco or Lustau's
vermut blanco will add more opulence
and depth.

VERMOUTH

BOULEVARDIER

◇◇◇◇◇◇◇◇◇◇◇◇◇◇◇◇◇◇◇◇◇◇◇◇◇◇◇◇

1 part Campari
1 part bourbon
1 part Martini Rosso or similar red vermouth
lemon peel, to garnish

Pour the Campari, whiskey and vermouth over ice in a rocks glass or tumbler and garnish with lemon peel.

This drink is attributed to Erskine Gwynne, 'cherub-faced and rumpus-raising' scion of the Vanderbilt clan, once the richest family in America. Like many Americans partial to a tipple and with the means to afford a ticket, Erskine left prohibition-era New York and crossed the Atlantic to raise rumpuses in the drinking dens of Europe. He moved to Paris where he frittered away his share of the family's fortunes by publishing a magazine called *Boulevardier*, named after the French word for a man-about-town frequenting fashionable boulevards and their bars at his leisure. Ostensibly *Boulevardier* was a 'literary' journal but in fact was more of a gossipy society mag aimed at dissolute expat boulevardiers such as Erskine himself.

Erskine drank at fellow New Yorker Harry MacElhone's eponymous Harry's New York Bar where he rubbed elbows with predictable regulars such as F. Scott Fitzgerald, Ernest Hemingway, Noël Coward and James Joyce, all of whom had work that appeared in the magazine. In his 1927 book *Barflies and Cocktails* Harry credits Erskine as inventing this drink.

The Boulevardier is essentially a Negroni where the gin is replaced with bourbon whiskey, giving the drink a macho depth invoking wood and leather. The original was equal measures of each ingredient, and that's what I prefer, although more modern recipes often double up on the bourbon. I see no reason not to use other whiskeys if that's what you've got to hand; in fact I prefer mine made with a peaty whisky such as Laphroaig which is less sweet than most bourbons and brings a pleasing smokiness to the drink.

AMERICANO SHANDY

//

Makes 2
25ml/1fl oz Campari
25ml/1fl oz red vermouth
330ml/12fl oz lager

Divide the Campari and vermouth between two glasses; the shape is up to you. Add ice and top up each glass with the lager, stirring gently to mix.

Are you mad? They said. Possibly,
I replied, but let's try it anyway.
Campari and sweet vermouth rub along
surprisingly well here with hoppy lager
to make a thirst-quenching shandy with
a certain Italian élan. Most beers come
in 330ml cans or bottles, just the right
amount to make two drinks.

I'm proud to say that Elliot Lidstone
and his partner Tessa put this drink
on the menu at their much-lauded
Box-E restaurant in Bristol. One could
not wish for higher approbation for
something that seemed a bit bonkers
but really works well.

ALBA ROSSA

|||||||||||||||||||||||||||||||||||||||||||||||||||||||||||

25ml/1fl oz rosé vermouth
75ml/3fl oz pink grapefruit juice
soda water
a few drops of grapefruit bitters (optional)

Stir together the vermouth and grapefruit juice over ice in whatever glass you think might suit. Top up with soda water and add grapefruit bitters to taste, if liked.

Rosé vermouths are a fairly new innovation, combining the red-berry fruitiness of their red cousins with the freshness of their white ones. Try Regal Rogue Wild Rosé, Belsazar Rosé or Cocchi Rosa in this. I'm not a massive fan of fruit juices in aperitifs but here pink grapefruit adds its own pleasing bitterness and the soda stops it being too sticky.

ADONIS

◇◇◇◇◇◇◇◇◇◇◇◇◇◇◇◇◇◇◇◇◇◇◇◇◇◇◇◇◇◇◇

15g/½oz coffee beans, plus a few extra, to garnish
250ml/10fl oz sweet vermouth (I like Martini Riserva Speciale Rubino)
250ml/10fl oz fino sherry (it also works with amontillado)
1 tsp orange bitters

Add the coffee beans to the vermouth, let them infuse at room temperature for about 15 minutes, then strain. Mix the vermouth with the sherry and pour into a clean bottle. Chill well, finishing it off in the freezer if you're in a hurry, then serve in small chilled glasses. Garnish with a coffee bean or three (odd numbers always seem to look more pleasing than even) if you like. This quantity makes 10 servings and will keep in a fridge for two weeks.

Allegedly invented in New York in 1884 in honour of the Broadway musical of the same name, the Adonis is a great mash up of two of my favourite things – sherry and vermouth. Some recipes call for more sherry than vermouth but I prefer equal measures. The coffee beans are not in the original recipe but are a clever addition given to me by drinks writer Richard Godwin; they give the drink a lovely depth but are a bit of a faff if you're only making a couple of drinks, which is why I tend to make up a batch using the above recipe and keep the bottle in the door of my fridge.

If you don't use the coffee beans, it's still a killer drink. Chill the vermouth and the sherry before you mix it, or quickly stir them over ice and strain into the glasses. A good 25ml/1fl oz each of sherry and vermouth makes a nice nip, but feel free to use more if you're in the mood for a stronger hit.

BAMBOO

//

1 part dry vermouth
1 part amontillado sherry
orange bitters

Mix up as an individual drink on the rocks, or stirred over ice if you can be bothered. Alternatively, mix up a batch in advance. Half a bottle each of vermouth and sherry and a teaspoon or thereabouts of orange bitters, mixed in a bottle and kept in the fridge to be served when and however you fancy it.

'One of the latest and most insidious drinks was recently introduced into swell saloons in this city by an Englishman. Consists of three parts sherry and one part vermouth. It is called "Bamboo" probably because after imbibing it the drinker feels like "raising Cain".' So the *St Paul Daily Globe* sanctimoniously pronounced in Minnesota in 1886, in one of the earliest references to this drink which mixes sherry and vermouth with such aplomb.

Recipes vary wildly: the sherry is sometimes fino, sometimes amontillado or occasionally a costly palo cortado, while both sweet and dry vermouths appear, sometimes both together. Here I take my lead from Felix Cohen at his wonderful bar Every Cloud in London, whose taste I trust implicitly. Felix favours Martini Extra Dry or Lillet Blanc as the vermouth, while Harvey's amontillado is his sherry of choice.

OTHER
SPIRITS

SEELBACH

◇◇◇◇◇◇◇◇◇◇◇◇◇◇◇◇◇◇◇◇◇◇◇◇◇◇◇◇◇◇◇◇◇

30ml/1fl oz bourbon
15ml/½fl oz triple sec or marmalade vodka (see page 75)
4 dashes Angostura bitters
Champagne or sparkling wine, chilled
orange twist, to garnish

**Mix the bourbon, triple sec and bitters in a chilled Champagne flute.
Top with Champagne and garnish with the orange twist.**

I was introduced to this by my friend Tom Hardwick, an Egyptologist who lives in Cairo, where he continues to unravel ancient mysteries a century after Howard Carter made his blockbuster discovery of Tutankhamun's tomb.

The Seelbach was the discovery of a young bartender called Adam Seger. In 1995, keen to make his name in the spirits world, Seger unearthed this recipe in the forgotten archives of the Seelbach Hotel in Louisville, Kentucky. Dating from pre-prohibition 1917, the drink was the result of a hapless bartender mistakenly mixing up a Champagne cocktail and a Manhattan that he was making for a newly wed couple, so creating what would become the hotel's signature drink.

This 'rediscovered' classic became an instant hit across the drinks world, its compelling backstory only adding to its decadent appeal, and it appeared in several authoritative cocktail books and journals over the following decades, including those by influential bartending gurus Gary Regan and Ted Haigh.

In 2016, Seger fessed up to Regan: there were no archives; the story was a myth. He'd first created the drink then invented the tale as a way to give it legitimate provenance and to put his name on the map. He had succeeded big time. Whether Seger confessed because he was unable to bear the burden of guilt any longer, or because he'd just opened his own bar in New York and could do with some publicity, is not recorded.

So this is not a genuine historical artefact, but it is a very, very good drink. Tom serves Seelbachs when he entertains in Egypt. His friends call it a Hardwick Wallbanger; you have been warned.

ROSE PETAL VODKA

|||||||||||||||||||||||||||||||||||||||||||||||||||||||||

Makes 1 bottle
6 heavily scented roses in the prime
   of bloom, freshly picked
1 bottle (70cl/25fl oz) vodka

Remove the petals from three roses, place in a glass or plastic container and pour over the vodka. Leave to infuse for 4 or 5 days, then remove the petals (the colour will have disappeared). Pick three more roses and add their petals to the vodka, leave for 4 more days, then strain and transfer to a clean bottle.

Rose petal vodka captures an English country garden in the summer and I'm indebted to food writer Felicity Cloake for this recipe from her lovely book *The A–Z of Eating*. Use the vodka to make a Martini with a gently flavoured vermouth – Belsazar Rosé makes a very charming pairing – or sip it alone very cold.

I frequently flavour vodkas, to drink alone or to use in cocktails. The process is very simple: add whatever you like to vodka, leave it to macerate for a few days then strain and put it into a bottle. Citrus peel and summer berries work particularly well, as do spices and woody herbs, perhaps used in conjunction with each other, sweetened or not according to your taste. Chilli vodka – slice a couple of red chillies vertically – gives an invigorating kick to a bloody Mary. Some people use sweets (candy) such as jelly beans or gummy bears; I would rather die.

RHUBARB MULE

◇◇◇◇◇◇◇◇◇◇◇◇◇◇◇◇◇◇◇◇◇◇◇◇◇◇◇◇◇

Makes 4
rhubarb juice (see below)
200ml/7fl oz vodka
about 600ml/21fl oz ginger beer
1 lime, cut into 4 wedges

To make the rhubarb juice:
750g/1lb 10oz rhubarb; trimmed and cut into chunks
juice and zest from 2 blood oranges
5cm/2in knob fresh finger; peeled and grated

For the juice, put the ingredients into a medium-sized pan over a gentle heat. Simmer for about 10 minutes, or until the rhubarb starts to collapse, stirring from time to time to prevent it sticking. Then, turn off the heat, cover with a lid and leave to cool.

Strain through a fine sieve and reserve the juice for the drink. Use the pulp to make a pudding – maybe a crumble or a fool – sweetened with sugar or maple syrup.

To make the drink, divide the rhubarb juice between four tall glasses – there should be about 50ml for each. Add a few cubes of ice and 50ml vodka, stir well, then top up with ginger beer. Squeeze the wedge of lime, then drop it into the glass and stir once more.

English rhubarb makes a welcome appearance in the dark days of post-Christmas winter, their jolly pink stalks so uplifting among the drab earthy colours of other local produce at that time of year. It happily coincides with blood orange season, for they make very happy partners.

Making the rhubarb juice is a bit of a faff so it's not really worth doing for fewer than four servings, but it does make the kitchen smell heavenly and you end up with the makings of an easy pudding, as well as a pretty, punchy aperitif.

MARMALADE VODKA

250g/9oz marmalade dregs
1 bottle (70cl/25fl oz) vodka

In a large pan gently heat the marmalade until it becomes liquid, then add the vodka and stir well.

Either put a lid on it and keep the pan in a cool dark place for two weeks, or transfer into sealed containers and do the same, stirring or shaking from time to time.

Use a fine sieve to strain into a large jug or jugs, then use a funnel to pour the marmalade vodka into clean bottles.

I don't make marmalade for the same reason I don't grow lettuces: I am fortunate to have friends who do it far better than I, and generously donate to me when they have a glut. Every January I gratefully receive several glowing jars of marmalade and have to clear out the dregs of last year's jars to make cupboard space for them. Marmalade Vodka is a noble finish to their lives, and makes a very cheering and versatile thing to have for so many things in the months to come.

Serve it over ice topped up with tonic or ginger beer for a thirst-quenching sundowner, or use it with a white vermouth to make a Martini, wet or dry. It can also be used to substitute triple sec, Cointreau or other orange-flavoured liqueurs in all manner of cocktails.

Sip it chilled as a shot, maybe with just one cube of ice, after dinner, or pour the shot over a fruity sorbet to give it a louche little kick. Hell, it even works when replacing the gin in a Negroni, what with orange being such a natural lover of Campari. Even better if an extra-dry white vermouth such as Noilly Prat replaces the usual Italian red, which keeps it from being too sweet.

OTHER SPIRITS

WHISKEY SODA

◇◇◇◇◇◇◇◇◇◇◇◇◇◇◇◇◇◇◇◇◇◇◇◇◇◇◇◇◇◇

about 50ml/2fl oz whiskey
about 200ml/7fl oz soda water

Pour the whiskey into a tumbler (see below), then add the soda water.

For me, brown spirits don't really fit into my frame of aperitif reference points – though I can quite see the appeal of a large bourbon on the rocks at the end of a heavy day, and of course a Mojito made well with good rum is a joyous thing if the day has also been hot.

But the Whiskey Soda was my grandfather's noggin (my grandmother preferred 'just a tiny sherry') and it holds a place in my heart for this reason. It does make a very good and easy aperitif, one of the simplest and most soothing there is. I spell it with an 'e' because my grandfather was Irish and Jameson was what he drank – only whiskies made in Scotland (or Japan) may be spelled 'whisky'. Choose whatever style of whiskey you like but this bashful drink doesn't demand anything special.

For me it's something to drink alone and contemplatively, quite possibly before and/or after a fish finger sandwich supper.

My grandfather always used a heavy, cut-glass tumbler, but anything that feels nice in your hand will do; choose a size to suit your thirst then add a couple of fingers of whiskey and four, no more, of soda water, ideally from an old-fashioned soda syphon. That's it. No ice.

MICHELADA

||||||||||||||||||||||||||||||||||||||||||||||||||||||||||||

juice of one lime, plus one wedge
large pinch of sea salt
lager – a Pilsner style works well
Tabasco or other hot sauce

Mix the lime juice and salt in a tall glass, add ice if you like, then top up with the beer and add hot sauce until it has the desired punch – 20 splashes of Tabasco does it for me. Squeeze the lime wedge over the top, drop it into the glass then drink. Ay caramba.

This lip-smacking thirst quencher turbo charges simple lager with a hairs-on-your-chest, lead-in-your-pencil kick of chilli, salt and lime. Originally hailing from Mexico, there is no hard-and-fast classic recipe; it's very much a drink to make to one's own taste. Some add tomato juice and/or Worcestershire sauce, but I think this takes it too far into the realms of being a beery Bloody Mary; soy sauce adds an extra whack of umami if you like that sort of thing.

You could wet the rim of the glass with water or lime juice and dip it into a saucer of ground chilli mixed with salt to really make your lips tingle, but it's a bit of a faff and detracts from the pleasing simplicity of the making. Any light beer or lager will do – but it's essential that it's very cold; if you chill your glass for 10 minutes in the freezer beforehand, so much the better. You can add ice to the drink but I prefer it without.

PIÑA COLADA

Makes 6
1 can pineapple chunks – about 450g/1lb
300ml/10½fl oz white rum
300ml/10½fl oz coconut cream
about 6 ice cubes
maraschino cherries, to garnish (optional)

Put the pineapple chunks – juice included – in a blender, add the other ingredients and blend until smooth. Serve in whatever glasses you have to hand and garnish with a maraschino cherry (and whatever else takes your fancy).

Please stand back as I don my leopard-print bikini, over-sized shades and plastic flower garland. Almost single-handedly, the Piña Colada (it means 'strained pineapple') kicked off the Great Cocktail Reboot of the late 1980s, its sweet and creamy exotic charms beloved by the ladz as well as the laydeez. Garnishes involving paper umbrellas, glacé cherries and straws shaped like flamingoes were favoured by its fans, and its starring roles in several lavish music videos of the time simply served to cement its popularity.

Snobs with a savoury palate mocked the PC as being the height of bad taste, in more ways than one. I'm ashamed to say I was one of those, but am now happy to correct the error of my ways. Few aperitifs are as kitsch as a PC, and they're definitely not for everyday drinking, but they make a very jolly start to a summery party with a Club Tropicana vibe.

DEATH IN THE AFTERNOON

//

25ml/1fl oz absinthe
125ml/4¾fl oz Champagne or sparkling wine

**Pour the absinthe into a flute and top up
with the Champagne or sparkling wine.**

Pray to the Lord for mercy.

This deliriously decadent drink
was allegedly invented by Ernest
Hemingway, which pretty much tells
you all you need to know. Champagne
and absinthe? What could possibly go
wrong?

MANZANILLA GIBSON

◇◇◇◇◇◇◇◇◇◇◇◇◇◇◇◇◇◇◇◇◇◇◇◇◇◇◇◇◇◇◇◇

25ml/1fl oz vodka
25ml/1fl oz manzanilla sherry
2 tsp juice from a jar of pickled silverskin onions

Stir the ingredients in a small glass with a few cubes of ice.

Strictly speaking, a Gibson is a Martini
(gin and dry vermouth) garnished with
a pickled cocktail onion and a splash of
its juice from the jar. Here, I substitute
manzanilla sherry for the vermouth, its
salty twang sitting very well against the
bracing sourness of the pickle juice.

A Gibson should properly be stirred
with ice, then strained into a chilled
cocktail glass, but I make mine in a
small tumbler on the rocks – partly
because I'm lazy, but also because the
dilution of the ice softens its hefty
thwack of alcohol. Rather than add an
onion to the drink, I prefer to serve
a few in a small bowl alongside it,
together with some ready-salted crisps.

WARM COSMOPOLITAN

Makes 4
100ml/4fl oz vodka
100ml/4fl oz triple sec or orange-flavoured liqueur
600ml/21fl oz cranberry juice
juice of two limes
orange twists and/or ground cinnamon, to garnish

Gently warm the ingredients in a small pan over a low heat – don't let the mixture boil. Divide between four heatproof glasses garnished with a twist of orange and/or a sprinkle of ground cinnamon.

I rather fell out of love with the Cosmopolitan many years ago, to be honest. They'd hit their heyday way back in the 1990s when Cosmopolitans became the trademark cocktail of the sassy women in TV's *Sex and the City*, by which time my tastes veered away from things overtly fruity to those with more of a bitter and/or sour personality. Served warm, however, I love them all over again as a cheery and welcoming aperitif on a cold winter's night.

They take minimal effort to make but because of the quantities involved, it seems barely worth it for fewer than four servings. You and a friend could always have a couple each should you find yourselves à deux, but there's no reason you couldn't make them individually in a glass then warm them in a microwave on a low setting.

It's worth recalling the scene at the end of the film adaptation of *Sex and the City* in 2008. 'Why did we ever stop drinking them?' asks Miranda. 'Because everyone else started,' Carrie replies. Perhaps it is now time to restore the Cosmopolitan, hot or cold, to its place on the aperitif catwalk.

VIN D'ORANGE

||||||||||||||||||||||||||||||||||||||||||||||||||||||||||||||

Makes 1.5 litres/2 pints 14fl oz
1 large orange, gently washed
20 cloves
1 litre/35fl oz unflavoured eau de vie
500ml/18fl oz sugar syrup (made by dissolving 500g/18oz sugar
* in 500ml/18fl oz of warm water)*

Stud the orange all over with the cloves, then put it in a glass or plastic bowl. Pour over the eau de vie. Cover and leave to infuse for 2 weeks. Transfer to a larger vessel and add the sugar syrup. Cover and set aside for a whole 2 months. Strain, chill, then drink. Très chic.

This is a really random recipe, given to me by a Frenchman who's better off forgotten. It's very simple but needs patience, much like the Frenchman himself, as it takes a couple of months from start to finish. It's a lovely thing to have in your fridge – it'll last for months – either to drink on its own or to fiddle around with; it adds a certain flair to cheap fizz that needs perking up and is also really, really good mixed with Campari or something similar on the rocks with a splash of soda.

KOMBUCHA MARGARITA

◇◇◇◇◇◇◇◇◇◇◇◇◇◇◇◇◇◇◇◇◇◇◇◇◇◇◇◇◇◇◇

50ml/2fl oz tequila
15ml/½fl oz triple sec or other orange liqueur
150ml/6fl oz kombucha
2 tsp cider vinegar (optional)
mint leaves, to garnish

Pour the tequila and triple sec over ice in a tall glass, then top up with kombucha of your choice – add the cider vinegar if you want to ramp up the sour. Garnish with a couple of mint leaves.

I arrived rather late to the kombucha party, not being sure that my life was long enough to embrace this drink: made from sweetened tea, kombucha is fermented with what's known as a SCOBY – a nifty acronym for 'symbiotic culture of bacteria and yeast'. Initially put off by its popularity among self-professed 'wellness gurus' who claimed all manner of improbably miraculous properties, I was eventually won round purely on aesthetic grounds.

Kombucha's sourness appeals to my savoury palate, and its slight effervescence makes it a natural candidate to be a mixer. Adding alcohol to it invariably makes it lose its virtuous health-giving glow, but one could almost argue that they cancel each other out. Here it sits very well with tequila, its sourness softer than that of the lime that is central to a classic margarita. Use whatever flavour of kombucha you prefer; I like those involving lemon and ginger.

PROVENÇAL OLD FASHIONED

50ml/2fl oz whiskey or bourbon
15ml/½fl oz pastis
4 dashes Angostura bitters (optional)
twist of lemon and a sprig of rosemary, to garnish

Mix the whiskey and pastis in a rocks glass filled with ice. Add the bitters, if using, stir once more, then garnish with the lemon and rosemary.

The classic Old Fashioned cocktail is made with sugar dissolved in Angostura bitters mixed with bourbon or rye whiskey over ice. It dates from the early 19th century when it was known simply as a Whiskey Cocktail but, as bartenders began to give their own 'twists' to the drink (as bartenders are wont to do) by including other spirits and liqueurs, customers faithful to the traditional ways of doing things started demanding them made in the 'old fashioned' way.

Absinthe appeared in one of these early 'twists' in Theodore Proulx's *Bartender's Manual* of 1888; here I've used pastis instead (but feel free to use absinthe if you have some) and eschewed the sugar altogether to suit more modern tastes. It makes a very distinctive aperitif for an autumn evening, the pastis bringing a liquorice sweetness to the woodiness of the whiskey while the lemon and rosemary give an astringent lift. I've called it 'Provençal' as a nod to these ingredients, but I very much doubt you'll find it on many menus on the French Riviera.

GREEN WALNUT RIKIKI

◇◇◇◇◇◇◇◇◇◇◇◇◇◇◇◇◇◇◇◇◇◇◇◇◇◇

Makes 2 litres/3½ pints
8 green walnuts, picked on or just before 14 July
500ml/18fl oz eau de vie
1.5 litres/2 pints 14fl oz red wine
500g/1lb 2oz sugar

Pierce each walnut through the middle with a knitting needle – it should go easily through the nut's skin without any resistance. Place in a large plastic container then pour over the eau de vie, ensuring the nuts are covered. Cover and leave for 3 weeks.

In a large saucepan, heat the red wine gently and add the sugar. Stir until the sugar has dissolved. Add the red wine syrup to the walnuts, cover and leave for 3 months. Drink over ice or as a warming tot on Bonfire Night or Thanksgiving.

You won't find rikiki on any internet search, or in any dictionary of booze; it seems it is particular to a little sleepy corner of the Dordogne/Charentes borders in France and refers to a drink made at home using local wine and eau de vie infused with nuts or fruit. The word may well be related to the Provençale verb *requinquilhar*, meaning to strengthen or to cheer up. It may also have something to do with the Spanish word *riquísimo*, meaning 'delicious', but then again it may not.

This recipe was given to me by an antiques dealer I met in a bar who carried a bottle of it around in his soft leather satchel. The recipe was given to him by his grandmother, who in turn inherited it from hers; it has rightfully stood the test of time. It's a slow burner – nearly four months from start to finish – but it's definitely worth the wait. It's dark as the devil with a captivating bittersweet warmth; make up a batch and sip it to lift the gloom of long winter nights.

GODFATHER

||||||||||||||||||||||||||||||||||||||||||||||||||||||||

35ml/1¼fl oz whiskey (Scotch or Irish; not too peaty)
15ml/½fl oz amaretto liqueur

Mix the ingredients in a rocks glass over ice.

I'm slightly ashamed of myself for liking this drink so much. Disaronno Amaretto sits in its chunky, sharp-shouldered bottle on the shelves of almost every bar in the world. Other brands are available but Disaronno, with its roots in 16th-century Renaissance Italy, is the best-selling brand of this tooth-achingly sweet, almond-flavoured liqueur and is the one most often found languishing stickily at the back of domestic cupboards.

Amaretto (meaning 'a little bitter', and not to be confused with amaretti biscuits made from ground almonds), hardly ever passes my lips, but this (supposedly one of Marlon Brando's favoured cocktails, hence its name) somehow strikes the right bittersweet balance as an occasional aperitif to bring out my inner gangster's moll.

This recipe makes a modest serving, which is usually enough for me. Replacing the whiskey with vodka makes the drink a Godmother; replacing it with brandy gives you a Godchild.

EARL GREY PUNCH

Makes six

400ml/14fl oz golden or dark rum
300ml/10½fl oz Earl Grey tea; 2 teabags brewed in
  about 500ml/17fl oz boiling water, then left to cool
100ml/4fl oz elderflower cordial
juice of two lemons
soda water

Stir the rum, tea, cordial and lemon juice in a large jug and add ice. Stir again, then top up with a little soda and serve in tall glasses. No garnish required.

This is my take on a Fish House Punch, supposedly invented in 1848 to celebrate women being allowed to join a fishing and social club known as the Fish House in Philadelphia, USA. The original uses peach liqueur but elderflower cordial is more easily available and adds a nicely fruity layer of flavour to the booze of the rum and the fragrant tannins of the tea.

MAURESQUE

//

35ml/1½fl oz pastis
25ml/1fl oz orgeat
about 100ml/4fl oz chilled water

Pour the pastis and orgeat into a tall glass and pour over the chilled water. Add ice cubes – adjust to taste with more water if liked, et Robert est votre oncle.

A pastis served in the classical way hits the spot for me almost every time, but if I do feel like a change and pretend I'm in a bar in the south of France, I might knock up a Mauresque.

The French are fond of their syrups and make them from almost anything that grows. They mix them with water to give to children and use them in drinks for grown-ups too. Orgeat is almond syrup and when mixed with pastis makes a very *ooh-la-la* sharpener for those with a penchant for anise.

If you replace the orgeat with grenadine (pomegranate syrup) you have a Tomate; strawberry syrup makes a pretty Rourou, while if you use crème de menthe you get a bright-green Perroquet.

INDEX

Managing Director: Sarah Lavelle
Assistant Editor: Sofie Shearman
Designers: Gemma Hayden and Emily Lapworth
Photographer: Sarah Hogan
Prop Stylist: Alexander Breeze
Copy Editor: Euan Ferguson
Head of Production: Stephen Lang
Senior Production Controller: Nikolaus Ginelli

First published in 2022 by Quadrille,
an imprint of Hardie Grant Publishing

Quadrille
52–54 Southwark Street
London SE1 1UN
quadrille.com

Cataloguing in Publication Data: a catalogue record for this book
is available from the British Library.

ISBN: 978 1 78713 879 7

Printed in China